# FENCES, GATES, AND WALLS

## E. ASHLEY ROONEY

PHOTOGRAPHY BY D. PETER LUND, UNLESS OTHERWISE CREDITED

Schiffer Publishing Ltd®

4880 Lower Valley Road   Atglen, Pennsylvania  19310

# ACKNOWLEDGMENTS

The commitment, care, and talent of my husband, D. Peter Lund, played a large role in my undertaking this book and the others preceding it . Before he died, my dad suggested I author books for Peter Schiffer and my husband take the necessary pictures. He thought that we would have the same fun that he had had. We have indeed!

Matthew Selby and Will Garrison of The Trustees of Reservations in Massachusetts played a major role in the creation of this book as did the enthusiasm of Angela Seaborg, Minglewood Designs, and the willingness of Knut Wefald, Robert Evans, and Siobhan Theriault to take yet-another picture of a wonderful fence.

**Photo credits:**
Front cover: *Long Hill, Andover, Massachusetts, a property of the Trustees of Reservations*
Spine:
Back cover: *Courtesy of Walpole Woodworkers*

Published by Schiffer Publishing Ltd.
4880 Lower Valley Road
Atglen, PA 19310
Phone: (610) 593-1777; Fax: (610) 593-2002
E-mail: Info@schifferbooks.com

For the largest selection of fine reference books on this and related subjects, please visit our web site at **www. schifferbooks.com**
We are always looking for people to write books on new and related subjects. If you have an idea for a book please contact us at the above address.

This book may be purchased from the publisher.
Include $3.95 for shipping.
Please try your bookstore first.
You may write for a free catalog.

In Europe, Schiffer books are distributed by
Bushwood Books
6 Marksbury Ave.
Kew Gardens
Surrey TW9 4JF England
Phone: 44 (0) 20 8392-8585; Fax: 44 (0) 20 8392-9876
E-mail: info@bushwoodbooks.co.uk
Website: www.bushwoodbooks.co.uk
Free postage in the U.K., Europe; air mail at cost.

Covers and book designed by: Bruce Waters
Type set in  Hallmark Black heading font/text font Ariel

ISBN: 978-0-7643-2643-1
Printed in China

# CONTENTS

*Courtesy of Tom Rider, California Redwood Assn.*

*Don't fence me in.*
*Let me ride through the wide open country that I love,*
*Don't fence me in.*
*Let me be by myself in the evenin' breeze,*
*Listen to the murmur of the cottonwood trees,*
*Send me off forever but I ask you please,*
*Don't fence me in.*
—Cole Porter, "Don't Fence Me In"
in the film Hollywood Canteen

# 1. FENCES, WALLS, AND NEIGHBORS

Walls and fences are part of our heritage. Even those early cave dwellers desired property, privacy, and safety. Over the years, as people wished to define their land boundaries, confine their livestock, provide security, or adorn the landscape, many different types of walls and fences have been developed— whether it be a stockade fence, a stonewall, or a hedge of thorns. Today, many of these walls are preserved and considered part of our heritage. Not only do they protect our house or gardens, but they also adorn our roads and fields.

Over time the language associated with walls and fences has become part of our idiom. We talk about "hitting a brick wall" or "sitting on the fence." We even had a President known as The Railsplitter.

Think of the metaphors. We talk about someone being "as solid as a brick" or "Just another brick in the wall." We can "come down on someone like a ton of bricks," be "up against the wall," or "go down the Yellow Brick Road." Then there's "solid as a rock" or "heart of stone." We can "hit the wall," "leave no stone unturned," or be "carved in stone." "The grass is always greener" (on the other side of the fence); we may be told to "mend our fences"; or find ourselves "fenced in." And everyone knows that "Good fences make good neighbors."

## Fences Over the Years

As tourists today, we might visit some famous old walls. We can climb the Great Wall of China or shake at our heads at the remains of the Berlin Wall. Walls are part of our lives. There's Hadrian's wall, the walls of Troy, Jericho, and the Kremlin, The Western or Wailing Wall in Jerusalem, The Atlantic Wall, Wall Street, Fenway Park's Green Monster in Boston, The Wall (the nickname for The National Vietnam Veterans Memorial in Washington, D.C) or Pink Floyd's album, "The Wall" ("All in all it's just another brick in the wall").

Tourists today know The Great Wall of China, which was built during the Ming Dynasty, starting around the year 1368 and lasting till around 1640. A massive defensive barrier, it was designed to protect the various dynasties from nomadic tribes. In 1987, the Wall was made a UNESCO World Heritage Site in 1987. *Courtesy of Knut Wefald*

4

Old walls, such as these at Delphi (Greece), follow the lay of the land, climbing steep hills, which leave today's tourists exhausted.

Initially constructed in August 1961, the Berlin Wall separated West Berlin from the rest of East Germany for 28 years in order to decrease emigration from East Germany. It physically divided the city and completely surrounded West Berlin. Part of the Iron Curtain, it was dismantled in the weeks following November 9, 1989. *Courtesy of Knut Wefald*

These Greek walls define different properties.

One definition of fence in many dictionaries is "to make a defense; to give protection or security, as by a fence." Originally, fences and walls were primarily for protection. We know from history that it took the Greeks ten years to figure out how penetrate Troy's walls. We marvel at the fragments of London wall on the grounds of the Museum of London and around Tower Hill. Built in the second century BC by the Romans, this wall helped to defend London from the Saxons in 457 A.D. and lasted until the nineteenth century. Even the twentieth century's Atlantic Wall was built by Hitler's orders to protect his Atlantic flank. To this day, fences are installed to protect property, children, and animals.

During the Middle Ages, especially in England, common lands began passing into private hands. Once community ownership dwindled and private property became more prevalent, fences began to appear, defining property ownership.

The first colonists to the New World knew the importance of fences. Without them, their animals would wander off or a neighbor's animals might wander in and decimate the crops. The kinds of materials available determined these early fences. The early New England colonists built stonewalls because the receding glaciers had left them an abundant supply of stones. Those in the southern and middle states used timber to make split rail or log fences. When those covered wagons carrying homesteaders reached the Prairies and Texas, entrepreneurs developed new forms of fencing, including a vast variety of barbed wire.

A fence at Hartwell Tavern on the Battle Road, Lexington, Massachusetts.

Walls and fences have become more popular today as our neighborhoods become more crowded, and homeowners require more privacy. A generation ago, backyards contained a hammock, some lawn chairs, and a portable charcoal grill. Today, many homeowners renovate their court or back yard to create an outdoor living room with comfortable furniture, built-in grill or complete kitchen, fire pit or fireplace, pool, and spa. Once they have furnished their outdoor rooms, homeowners are loath to sit on their expensive new furniture and look at their neighbor's garage or listen to a barking dog. In self defense, they may erect a fence or a wall.

New England fence and barn at Old Sturbridge Village photographed by Angela Kearney, Minglewood Designs. *Used with permission of Old Sturbridge Village*

## Fences Today

There are many reasons why we install a wall or fence. You can have a fence as a decoration (think of those cute upright white pickets), to hide an ugly view (such as the air conditioning unit), to enclose the swimming pool, or to create a sound buffer. Good fences require good design and some thought. Sometimes, wall and fence design is driven by function; enclosing children or a prize pet in the back yard is certainly different from concealing the spa. A fence or wall can define boundaries or accent surroundings. Sometimes you want a fence or wall to blend into the background; sometimes you want it to make a statement.

Adding a wall or fence to your property can be an overwhelming decision. Today, a range of styles and designs, multiplied by a variety of materials and quality grades, exists.

If you are unsure of what kind of wall or fence you require, first determine your reasons for installing a fence.

Are you looking for a decorative touch or do you want to provide some privacy? Do you need the fence to protect your swimming pool from wandering toddlers or to block out your neighbor's back yard? Or are you trying to protect your property from wandering animals? Before considering a specific style, you must first decide whether it is a practical choice for your home. If the purpose of the fence is to contain an animal (or keep one out), you may need a high mesh fence. On the other hand, if you are looking for a fence to define your property and provide a welcoming feeling for visitors, then a three-foot picket fence might do the trick.

Generally, the more basic the house, the more straight forward the fence should be. You certainly don't want towering stonewalls surrounding a simple ranch or Cape. White picket fences fit New England; redwood suits the Western states. The fence should match the scale and appearance of the house. A good rule of thumb is to consider using the same material as the siding of your house.

Before laying a foundation or calling that contractor, talk to your neighbors. By asking them their opinion, you make them part of the project; as a result, they may consider the addition of a fence more favorably. Then check with your local building officials regarding the zoning ordinances and building codes that specify the style of fence you can build, how high it can be, and how far it must be kept from the property line or street. They will tell you whether a building permit is required. They may even tell you whether you can build a fence on your site.

To determine where your fence should be located, draw your property to scale, including bordering property, public land such as sidewalks and roads, access, and buildings. Mark the distance of your house from property lines and designate setback lines and other limitations as required by applicable zoning regulations. You can use this plan as part of your application, if a permit is required.

This stonewall runs the length of the property. Behind it stands a living hedge of evergreens, giving it a multi-dimensionality.

This lattice fence obscures the view in and out of the garden.

Not only does this brick serpentine wall provide privacy, but it also blocks street noise and headlights.
*Long Hill, Andover, Massachusetts, a property of the Trustees of Reservations.*

A redwood fence encloses this small Virginia courtyard.

When evaluating a fence and its cost, consider how long you want it to last. Is this a product that will last ten years? How much maintenance does it require? A well chosen fence should enhance your home and add to its value.

Once you have defined the fence's role, your preferred style, and budget, you need to choose the right fence for the job. In most instances, a fence defines space, creates privacy, and provides shelter and shade. Ideally, it is beautiful, offering style and utility to your home. You have a range of possible options:

- Boundary fences enhance the appearance of a property or garden. Typically low and simple, a boundary fence can remind the kids about the perimeter of your yard.
- Privacy fences are designed to block the view from the outside and inside. These fences have become increasingly popular as homeowners have begun to use their patios, decks, and pool areas as outdoors leisure space.
- Security fences prevent trespassing or theft and/or keep children and pets from wandering away.

Of course, once you have installed your fence, you may wish to contemplate a gate.

## Boundary Fences

In the late 1800s, a decorative wrought iron or elaborate wood fence often surrounded the front lawn of a Victorian home. The fence acted as the framing for this outdoor room that provided a place for the family to meet guests and entertain in a manicured landscape. In successive decades, the front yard became less important and received less attention. In the last twenty years, as the suburbs have become more crowded, white pickets and split rails have returned to the suburban neighborhood.

Boundary fences are attractive additions to a property. They create an image or visual impact more than they secure or protect. By adding a fence, a homeowner can break the monotony of a long stretch of backyard against the woods. Using the fence as a background for a small garden or as support for climbing flowers or vines is even more dynamic.

A boundary fence can have a major impact on the perception of your house and the appearance of the neighborhood. Ideally, a fence appears attractive and welcoming. It is a low fence (approximately four feet) that marks the property edges. A good boundary fence isn't offensive to the neighbors, but it does prevent the neighborhood children from cutting across your lawn!

Many residences turn to strong, durable chain link fencing, which requires little or no maintenance and costs less than a wood fence. Its light, airy appearance won't block the view, cast deep shadows, or affect the neighbors as much as most wood fences. And if you don't like its appearance, you can easily screen it with climbing plants or bushes. A more attractive chain link that's coated with green or black vinyl is available at a cost of about 20 percent more than uncoated steel.

If you intend to landscape (which we would urge), a wood fence or a fence made from a material that's consistent with your home is a good choice. The fence will become a landscaping feature and accent your home as well.

## Privacy Fences

As the American landscape gets increasingly built up, privacy is a serious concern. We may enjoy chatting with our neighbors, but we prefer to talk to our family without the whole neighborhood looking on. Most of us want our homes to be a place where peace can be enjoyed at the end of our hectic day. Frequently, our homes border our neighbors' or the busy street with its traffic noise, and we may not have that much-desired privacy.

Privacy fences can substantially enlarge the outside living space of the home. By adding a fence, you can transform your property into functional outdoor rooms, which you can enjoy without being visible to the entire neighborhood. A high solid fence is the usual choice, but a thick row of hedges can also meet this need.

Privacy fences block out the trash cans, the neighbor's yard, the noisy streets, the nosy neighbors and enhance our security. They also enclose our home, block our property from view, and act as wind and sound barrier. These new areas can give us a special, intimate place where we can relax and reflect, sheltered from the cares of the world. As oases from our responsibilities inside the home, these become whimsical and playful, spacious and cozy places in our hectic lives.

Unfortunately, a privacy fence has a major impact on your neighbors and the community, especially if you build it at or near the boundaries of your property. It obscures the neighbor's view, blocks the sun or cooling breezes, ruins a flowerbed, or comes too close to a neighbor's house. For these reasons, municipalities often regulate fence design through building codes, limiting their height, their "setback" from the property line, and even their appearance. In other words, in designing a fence, you should be a good neighbor and consider your neighbor's interests as much as possible in your design!

A privacy fence doesn't have to be solid to create privacy. It can be designed in a staggered board or basket weave style or a combination of solid boards topped with lattice, which provides some visibility over the top while allowing breezes to pass through. Such a privacy fence is not only visually attractive but also effective.

A living fence or a wall of bushes and trees can make a fine privacy screen, although you'll have to wait several years for the plants to grow high enough with thick branches and foliage to screen out the outside world. It can act as a partition to enclose an area or to conceal the children's playground. Just a single section of fence can make a big difference.

## Security Fences

When a new puppy arrives, when the kids are young and you want to keep them in sight, or when you want to protect the garden, style considerations usually take a back seat to low cost and ease of installation.

A security fence aims to discourage potential intruders (human or animal) from going over, under, or through the structure. Height and sharp edges can deter property theft and vandalism, while strength and proper placement can discourage animals. Although many types of fence can be used for security, local building ordinances may affect the allowable height and design. You don't want to block a neighbor's view or obstruct a light source. A security fence should be six to eight feet tall, depending on the intruders you're trying to keep out. If privacy isn't an issue, an open design will allow air to circulate through your yard. It also will keep the fence from becoming the dominant feature in your landscape.

The word wall usually refers to barriers made from solid brick or concrete, blocking vision as well as passage, while a fence is a freestanding and lighter structure. The definitions overlap somewhat. In the following chapters, we treat walls separately and discuss fences according to function.

*"Do not protect yourself by a fence, but rather by your friends."* Norman Vincent Peale.

Decorated for the holidays, this ornamental iron fence certainly protects the property behind it.

This chain link fence sports a wisteria garland.

A Walpole Woodworkers fence encloses this beautiful pool. *Courtesy of Walpole Woodworkers*

# 2. MASONRY WALLS

Many people consider walls constructed of stone, brick, concrete, or combinations of masonry types to be solid, dependable, and permanent. Certainly, masonry is associated with many beautiful structures such as the Acropolis and the great European cathedrals.

Masonry is often chosen for its unique patterns, textures, and colors, its economy, and its ability to withstand natural disasters. As a construction process, it can be carried out with small, relatively inexpensive tools on the construction site. It can be designed to support structural loads and to resist water penetration and heat transfer.

The major problem with masonry walls – other than being destroyed by man or machine – is that they expand and contract as temperature and moisture change. Water running down a masonry wall, for example, can collect in its joints, where freezing and thawing cycles can gradually spall off the mortar. Once the mortar is damaged, the wall is weakened. To prevent this process, the mason should apply a suitable weather-resistant mortar and fill the joints tightly.

## Stonewalls over the Ages

Dry-stacked stonewalls, constructed from stones stacked atop one another without mortar or other adhesives, were being constructed before history was being recorded. Old stonewalls can be found through the world.

From ancient to modern times, most cities built walls as a fortification and to resist sieges. In Greece today, you can see remains of walls built many centuries before. Some walls, such as the Great Wall of China and Hadrian's Wall, enclosed regions or signaled territorial boundaries. Some incorporated rivers or other topographic elements in order to make the wall more effective. Many of these walls also symbolized the status and independence of the communities they embraced.

*"Joshua fought the battle of Jericho,*
*Jericho, Jericho,*
*Joshua fought the battle of Jericho*
*And the walls came tumbling down."*

Stonewall and gate at Old Sturbridge Village photographed by Angela Kearney, Minglewood Designs. *Used with permission of Old Sturbridge Village*

11

The ancient Greeks considered Delphi to be the center of the world. Today, visitors follow in the footsteps of the ancient pilgrims to the site, winding their way up the hillside to the Temple of Apollo.

Archaeological excavations began around 1900. Many archeologists and students have labored to rebuild these walls built upon walls.

A stonewall was a common field boundary during the Medieval Age in Europe. When landowners abandoned farming in favor of livestock, they began to enclose the common grazing lands. As rough irregular stonewalls enclosed the fields, the villagers' right to use the land was lost.

When the colonists arrived in the New World from Europe, they found a rugged environment with swamps and rocks impeding their need to carve a living out of the land. Not only did they face the wild life and a strange new country, but they also had to clear the land. Practical pioneers, they used the stones to create fieldstone walls or "thrown" walls to keep their livestock and crops safe. Thrown stonewalls wander throughout the New England countryside.

In other parts of Greece, homeowners just incorporate the ancient walls into their properties.

Even today, you can see miles upon miles of stonewalls marching through the New England woods, hearkening back to the seventeenth century. These dry stonewalls suit the landscape because the material is taken right from the ground.

Unlike many other types of fences, which may rot and must be replaced every 10-15 years, stone does not. Robert Thorson, a University of Connecticut geology professor, says, "Stone walls are important because they are signal flags for history and prehistory, the threads that hold the historic landscape together." In his book, *Exploring Stone Walls* (Walker & Company, 2005), he states that many New England stonewalls were built in the late eighteenth and early nineteenth centuries and that the use of concrete mortar wasn't prevalent until after the Civil War.

Some builders were good stonemasons, and some weren't.

*"Something there is that doesn't love a wall,*
*That sends the frozen-ground-swell under it*
*And spills the upper boulder in the sun,*
*And make gaps even two can pass abreast."*
—*Robert Frost, "Mending Wall"*

A stonewall in front of Hartwell Tavern on the Battle Road in Lexington, Massachusetts. In Pre-Revolutionary days, travelers to and from Boston stopped at Hartwell Tavern, visited, and talked about what was going on in the world. Early on April 19, 1775, Dr. Samuel Prescott reached Hartwell Tavern, to alert the Lincoln Minutemen about the oncoming British.

Some can tell the age of the wall from the signs of collapse and amount of lichen on the wall.

Subsequent generations rebuilt these early stonewalls, creating more formal walls, which emphasized stability and beauty. These walls became part of the landscape design.

Building with stone requires a substantial commitment of time and effort. A thrown stonewall is easier to build than a mortared stonewall. The friction and the weight of the stacked stones hold the stones together.

In this twentieth century dry stonewall, random stones and pebbles have been used to shim unleveled stones and prevent soil from seeping through the wall. *Courtesy of Phil Rossington*

A mortared wall, however, does well in heavily traveled areas and is durable, if it has a footing. Without a footing, it may crack because of settling or frost heaves.

A "dry" stonewall has no mortar holding it together. It relies on gravity and friction to maintain its shape and integrity. Automatically self draining, it does not need a separate concrete footing. People sitting on it, the odd soccer ball, or traffic vibration can damage it.

*"I want you to stonewall it, let them plead the Fifth Amendment."*
                    *—Richard M. Nixon*

Stonewalls are often used for retaining walls, which hold back the soil, permitting an abrupt change in grade without causing erosion.

Stonewalls highlight landscapes.

They reinforce the property lines.

They frame exuberant mixtures of annuals and perennials.

A stonewall is not only charming but also long lasting. They do require occasional maintenance. *Courtesy of Knut Wefald.*

Stonewalls can be build with or without mortar, depending on the desired appearance, strength, and purpose. A well built stonewall will require little, if any, maintenance and should outlive its builder. It is also durable, attractive, and virtually maintenance free.

This series of retaining walls enhances a hillside with planted terraces. *Naumkeag, Stockbridge, Massachusetts, a Property of the Trustees of Reservations*

The perennial planting and containers of annuals soften this cedar picket fence and stone retaining wall. *Courtesy of Brian Cossari, ASLA – Hoffman Landscapes, Inc.*

Generally, a retaining wall is one foot or more in height. If it is about two feet in height, it not only retains the soil but also act as a bench. A wall less than twelve inches or so as seen here is called a curb. *Naumkeag, Stockbridge, Massachusetts, a Property of the Trustees of Reservations*

Our forefathers could gather up the loose stones lying in the fields and use them. Any New England gardener will tell you that their gardens grow their own stones. Today, however, many good sources of stones have dried up. You may have an old wall on your property that could be used, but then you are destroying that relic from the past. You may have a friend who is digging a garden or find some rocks at a construction site, but you should first ask.

You can also purchase stone. In most cases, select stones that are native to your area . Stone is usually sold by the ton. A stone dealer should be able to give you an idea of how much you need.

The down side of stonewalls is that stone is heavy, hard to transport, and irregular in shape.

The bigger stumbling block is finding the stone and the builder.

## Types of Stone

Natural stone is a generic term for any quarried and cut stone that is used for construction purposes. The actual types of stone include granite and various kinds of limestone, which all have slightly different aesthetic differences.

**Rubble** or **fieldstone** is rough and irregular and gives an informal look. Rubble comes from a quarry; fieldstone stone is gathered in fields and from dried up riverbeds. The latter is the best choice for traditional rock walls. Usually masses of irregular rough pieces, the stones are trimmed when necessary, to fit against each other. Rubble masonry may be coursed or un-coursed, dry laid, or laid in mortar. A more formal or architectural appearance is created by cut stone or by stones with naturally flat planes that fit together neatly such as slate and some limestone.

**Ashlars,** "**dressed stone**" or "**cut stone**," is also a quarried stone product, but it is cut into more consistent rectangular blocks. Because it gives the mortar a smooth flat surface, it works well in mortared walls or as a facing for a wall. The stones are laid in courses similar to mortared brick, and the joints are finished in a similar way.

**Trimmings** are cut stone used to form special courses, moldings, bases, or copings for walls. These stones are usually cut in matched lengths from two to four feet in length, match marked so that they may be placed in the order that they were cut, and fastened together by means of iron dowels in the joints.

Note the square-cut base mid-way up the stone pillar.

Charles Prowell Woodworks designed a series of woven grid panels to soften the stone knee walls and columns. *Courtesy of Charles Prowell*

This multi-dimensional backdrop (wall, fence, and plantings) augments the landscape design.

Stonewalls assume a different character when they become a backdrop for plantings.

When flowers are planted in pockets of soil in a dry stonewall, the wall becomes a multicolored sculpture.

## Brick

One of the world's oldest building materials, bricks have been in use for more than five thousand years. These small, rectangular blocks are usually made of clay that has been kiln dried for strength, hardness, and heat resistance.

This long Greek wall fortifies the hillside.

The substantial brick wall accentuates the length of Bellevue Avenue in Newport, Rhode Island.

Roman legions, which operated mobile kilns, introduced bricks to many parts of the empire. The legion that supervised the brick's production often stamped their mark on the brick. Brick walls were unpopular during the Renaissance and the Baroque periods so plaster often covered brickwork until the mid-eighteenth century.

Brick walls have many different patterns and textures.

*"A common, ordinary brick wants to be something more than it is."*

—*Woody Harrelson, "Indecent Proposal."*

In the late 1800s, Caroline and Joseph Hodges Choate, a prominent New York attorney and U.S. Ambassador to the Court of St. James, decided to build a summer estate in the village of Stockbridge, Massachusetts, known today for its connection with Tanglewood, the summer home of the Boston Symphony Orchestra, and many other organizations. Designed by McKim, Mead & White in 1885 and completed in 1886, the Choate home belongs to a class of luxurious summer homes that are happily known as "summer cottages." Choate called it Naumkeag, the native name for his birthplace, Salem, Massachusetts. Mabel Choate, their second daughter, inherited the property in 1929. She and landscape architect Fletcher Steele concentrated on the gardens and the landscaped areas. When she died in 1958, she bequeathed Naumkeag and its contents to the Trustees of Reservations who continue to make the house and its gardens open to the public.

There are dramatic brick arches. *Naumkeag, Stockbridge, Massachusetts, a Property of the Trustees of Reservations*

Today, Naumkeag is famous for its eight acres of terraced gardens and landscaped grounds surrounded by forty acres of woodland, meadow, and pasture that stretch to the Housatonic River Valley. *Naumkeag, Stockbridge, Massachusetts, a Property of the Trustees of Reservations*

Naumkeag includes many fascinating garden "rooms" enclosed by brick garden walls. *Naumkeag, Stockbridge, Massachusetts, a Property of the Trustees of Reservations*

Brick garden walls are marvelous backdrops for landscaping.

Brick walls make great privacy walls, blocking out the hum of tires, the fire engine siren, and the sporadic glare of headlights from passing cars. They also help to inhibit curious tourists in Newport, Rhode Island.

This serpentine wall acts a sound barrier for an estate on a busy intersection in Cambridge, Massachusetts. Unfortunately, several cars have run into it, damaging its massive curves and probably destroying the automobile. If you look carefully, you can see where it has been repaired.

Brick walls are often adorned with vines, which soften the harshness of the material.

Frequently, other materials are incorporated in the brick wall to accentuate their solid simplicity.

*"Bricks and mortar make a house, but the laughter of children makes a home."*

*—Irish Proverb*

The use of bricks in construction is common – particularly in regions that lack stone or other construction materials. During the building boom of the nineteenth century in the eastern United States, bricks were used in construction because of their cost, flexibility, strength, and appearance. During the early twentieth century, modern architects and theorists advocated the use of more sophisticated materials such as glass or steel rather than brick. Nevertheless, brick continued to be used.

Building a brick wall can be expensive and labor intensive, but it will last a long time and can carry a considerable load. A brick wall is mortared and can have different patterns, colors, and textures.

The bricks are laid in rows called courses. They can be laid to expose their ends (header bricks) or sides (stretcher bricks). Today, the most common type of brickwork is the simple stretcher bond (also known as running bond or monotonous stretcher bond), where only the long side surface of the brick is shown. The manner in which the bricks overlap is called the bond. Types of bond include English, Flemish, and Herringbone.

This impressive column lends a feeling of solidity to the end of the low fence. The grapevine mortar joint, extruded brick with rough surface texture, and a whitewash-type coating refer to older design and construction in brick masonry. *Courtesy of the Brick Industry Association*

The entry to this plantation-style house features steps and a retaining wall of antiqued brick. The molded brick look harkens back to days when brick were hand made on site. *Courtesy of the Brick Industry Association*

A blind arch, moved forward of the wall plane, provides an interesting appeal to this retaining wall. The projected keystone of cut brick adds more shadows. The herringbone pattern beneath the arch further demonstrates the artistic features of brickwork. The texture of the antiqued brick emphasizes the handmade look. *Courtesy of the Brick Industry Association*

Brick columns and wainscots along with in fill panels of brick add privacy and an earth tone background to the plants at these botanical gardens in St. Louis. Flemish bond, courses of alternating stretchers and headers, are used in the columns and wainscot. The diamond pattern brickwork in the panel mimics the grid in the woodwork between other columns. Garden beds are raised within a surround of brickwork. *Courtesy of the Brick Industry Association*

If good fences make good neighbors, the neighbors in Lubbock, Texas, must be among the best! Brick privacy walls separate many residential developments from the streets, thus muting the street noise. The single brick thick fence sections span between columns and may be constructed without a continuous foundation, as shown here. *Courtesy of the Brick Industry Association*

The variety of masonry treatments on the top of the fences and columns, along with different brick colors, keep a fresh, unifying look to the neighborhoods. *Courtesy of the Brick Industry Association*

Laid in running bond and with wire reinforcing in the mortar joints, these fences are most economical. *Courtesy of the Brick Industry Association*

This brickwork gateway proudly ushers residents and guests to this subdivision in North Carolina. The brick is laid in Flemish bond. Specially shaped brick top the wall in smoothly curved surfaces. *Courtesy of the Brick Industry Association*

Privacy and lightness are hallmarks of brick screen walls. Recessing the central portion reduces the bulk of the columns. Lights and plants on alternate columns lift the eye. *Courtesy of the Brick Industry Association*

## Concrete

Concrete walls offer strength, ease of upkeep, and a wide variety of customized looks. Decorative or architectural concrete block can create handsome, freestanding walls.

Often, block walls are finished with plaster, stucco or, in the case of buildings and perimeter walls, with various forms of cladding to create an appealing aesthetic.

Inexpensive, easy to lay and durable, modular concrete units are available in a range of decorative styles.

Concrete masonry became popular in the early twentieth century because of the expense and scarcity of competing materials. Moreover, concrete blocks could be locally manufactured using readily available materials.

Concrete walls are not usually a do-it-yourself project. Installation often requires masonry skills and an understanding of such factors as weight, wall base preparation, and landscape drainage. Improper preparation and installation can drastically reduce the lifespan of the wall, and repairs can be expensive.

In recent years, the use of concrete components has evolved considerably.

This elaborate concrete wall protects a large Newport estate.

These concrete privacy walls provide a sense of personal space.

Park Slope Design created a courtyard to complement the Spanish style architecture and to provide the owners with an outdoor sitting area in the front of the home. *Courtesy of Joan Grabel/Park Slope Design*

The aim of this Park Slope Design project was to create a courtyard in the front yard of this Spanish home in Beverly Hills, California. Previously, the house had just a typical front yard border. *Courtesy of Joan Grabel/Park Slope Design*

**40**

White stucco walls that match the house surround the courtyard. The wrought iron patina-style gate was custom built to match the existing wrought iron on the upper balcony. *Courtesy of Joan Grabel/Park Slope Design*

These walls have a Mediterranean feel.

In an effort to offer both privacy and aesthetics for a renowned novelist, Charles Prowell Woodworks added some ironwork to the gate to complement the Mediterranean architecture. *Courtesy of Charles Prowell*

A solid privacy and sound wall encloses this sprawling property. To reduce the impression of an unfriendly fortress, the wall is relieved with an occasional Charles Prowell Woodworks fence panel. *Courtesy of Charles Prowell*

The matching garden and drive gates also create some much-needed relief. *Courtesy of Charles Prowell*

A solid masonry wall flanks this solid garden gate designed by Charles Prowell Woodworks. *Courtesy of Charles Prowell*

The climbing vines adorn the walls, adding a softening touch. *Courtesy of Charles Prowell.*

# 3. BOUNDARY FENCES

In the late 1800s, a decorative, low, wrought iron or elaborate wood fence often surrounded the front lawn of a Victorian home. A fence would frame this manicured environment, where the family met and entertained guests. In successive decades, a fence in the front of the house made little sense, particularly as homes became more informal. As America has become increasingly built up, the white pickets and split rails have returned to the suburban landscape, and homeowners are marking their boundaries more frequently.

A "boundary" fence is a fence that marks the property edges and that is low enough to see over (approximately four feet). It is the type of fence you install when you want to accentuate an ambiguous property line or to prevent the newspaper delivery person from cutting through your lawn. A good boundary fence is just high enough to do the job but doesn't try to shut out the neighborhood.

Boundary fences are attractive additions to a property. They create an image and provide visual impact more than they secure or protect. They can have a major impact on the perception of your house and the appearance of the neighborhood. A length of fence can interrupt the monotony of a long stretch of backyard. An even more exciting strategy is to use the fence as a background for a small garden or as support for some climbing flowers or vines. Ideally, it appears attractive and welcoming.

Many mansions use cast iron or aluminum fences, which are quite formal (see Chapter 5). Other residences turn to strong, durable chain link fencing, which requires little or no maintenance and usually costs less than a wood fence.

If you have ambitious ideas for landscaping, a wood or vinyl fence is a better choice. It'll accent your home and become a landscaping feature as well.

Natural wood is the preferred material in many areas. It is available, affordable, and easy to work with. It complements all types of properties and has an endless number of styles. On the other hand, wood requires significant maintenance. It is affected by moisture, temperature variations, insects, and sunlight. It requires that coat of paint or stain.

During the last ten years, the vinyl or PVC fence has become an attractive alternative. These strong and environmentally sturdy fences come in several colors and a range of styles, including picket, basket weave, three-rail, and lattice. Generally, they look just like wood. They offer attractiveness, sturdiness, and ease of maintenance. A vinyl fence does not rot or have to be painted; it just needs the occasional power washing.

One of the most highly valued benefits is the warranty available for vinyl. Because it is rot resistant and needs no painting, vinyl fences come with extensive warranties, and many manufacturers even offer lifetime warranties.

Fences generally fall into five basic styles with many variations:

1. Board or panel fencing
2. Louvered or lattice fencing
3. "Good neighbor" fencing
4. Post and rail fencing
5. Picket fencing

There is also something known as decorative fencing, which is just a furbelow or a way of providing an easy screen.

## Board or Panel Fencing

A solid, private barrier appeals to many homeowners. This type of fence provides privacy and can also protect against wind and street noise.

Fitch Tavern, Bedford, Massachusetts, has a lovely white picket fence. Twenty-six minutemen gathered there on the morning of April 19, 1775, following the alarm that the British were on the march from Boston. Captain Jonathan Wilson looked at his men and said, "It is a cold breakfast, boys, but we'll give the British a hot dinner; we'll have every dog of them before night." The Minutemen then marched on foot to Concord for the battle at the bridge.

Orchard at Old Sturbridge Village photographed by Angela Kearney, Minglewood Designs. *Used with permission of Old Sturbridge Village*

The diagonal fence boards add a touch of lightness to the solid box-like design of this screen divider. Knot-containing garden grades of redwood, Construction Heart and Construction Common, are ideal for a structure of this type. *Courtesy of Ernest Braun, California Redwood Assn.*

The height of this fence screens out street sights and sounds. The spacing of the boards can be varied to accommodate a specified amount of airflow and privacy. Built of clear grade redwood, the contrasting sapwood-heartwood content adds color interest. *Courtesy of Rufus Diamant, California Redwood Assn.*

A rustic fence of Construction Heart redwood defines this property line. The fence is personalized with built-in benches and planters to add extra beauty and livability to the property. The trellis-shaded fence provides maximum privacy and protection from wind while serving as an attractive support for flowering vines. *Courtesy of Karl Riek, California Redwood Assn.*

A Construction Common deck is enhanced by a set of twin trellises with a sloping design. Built-in benches and the redwood fence complete the attractive setting. *Courtesy of Ernest Braun, California Redwood Assn.*

This fence style from Walpole Woodworkers harkens back to the stockade fencing of the past. *Courtesy of Walpole Woodworkers*

## Lattice or Louvered Fencing

A louvered or lattice fence offers some interesting play with light. Lattice panels can be arranged in a choice of designs and patterns to complement your planting decisions and individual sense of style. Many suppliers offer, in addition to various lattice styles, a modular panel system that allows you to select the base panel and top panel of your choice.

This latticework boundary fence compliments a turn-of-the century white cottage and English garden design. The posts are shaped at the top to add architectural interest. *Courtesy of Ernest Braun, California Redwood Assn.*

The disparity between a lattice fence and a flush-joined grid are exemplified in this Charles Prowell Woodworks' original. *Courtesy of Charles Prowell*

Classic redwood lattice panels surround the deck. *Courtesy of Ernest Braun, California Redwood Assn.*

This privacy screen adds visual interest to the back yard. The louvered construction is a sophisticated way to let in light and breezes while maintaining privacy. *Courtesy of Jeff Weissman, California Redwood Assn.*

Landscaping obscures the view in or out of this elegant Walpole Woodworkers lattice fence. *Courtesy of Walpole Woodworkers*

This Charles Prowell Woodworks original is a landscape-friendly design of lower mortised pickets and upper joined grids. *Courtesy of Charles Prowell*

This combination fence from Walpole Woodworkers carefully frames this Victorian garden. *Courtesy of Walpole Woodworkers*

A Walpole Woodworkers fence carefully screens this gated entrance to the rear of the property. *Courtesy of Walpole Woodworkers*

This long boundary fence separates one back yard from another. *Courtesy of Walpole Woodworkers*

## "Good Neighbor" Fencing

This board-on-board fence promises privacy and, concurrently, defines the property borders. More importantly, it looks as good on the outside as it does on the inside, thus pleasing the neighbors.

This picket-style fence draws a firm but attractive line on this Annapolis, Maryland, street.

This seven-foot high, redwood fence buffers traffic noise on a busy main street. The massive stockade-like design is a board-on-board or "Good Neighbor" style that looks nice from either side. *Courtesy of Tom Rider, California Redwood Assn.*

Thanks to these "Good Neighbor" styles, both you and your neighbor get to look at the "good" side.
*Courtesy of Walpole Woodworkers*

## Post and Rail Fencing

Post and rail is especially good for a long boundary fence. Its open casual look helps it to blend invisibly with the background. Generally inexpensive, it is easy to build (if you are into playing home handyman) and can augment a variety of home and garden styles.

*"I'm just sittin' on a fence*
*You can say I got no sense*
*Trying to make up my mind*
*Really is too horrifying*
*So I'm sittin on a fence."*
    —The Rolling Stones, "Sitting on a Fence,"
        in the album Flowers

Post and rail styles of fencing are often found on ranches and farms. Because it uses less wood than other styles of fencing, post and rail fencing covers large amounts of land economically. It also provides a safe way to contain livestock. Rolling fence, Old Sturbridge Village photographed by Angela Kearney, Minglewood Designs. *Used with permission of Old Sturbridge Village*

The post and rail or split rail fence is an American classic.

A three-rail fence produces a fence between four and five feet high.

Generally, a split rail fence is composed of two rails, making the fence about three feet high.

Rot-resistant woods such as cedar or pressure-treated fir can increase the life of your fence.

Like most fences, the post and rail has its variations. *Courtesy of Walpole Woodworkers*

## Picket Fencing

When we think of fences, we usually think of the low, open, white picket fence. A picket fence certainly doesn't fit every home –certainly not the McMansion or a contemporary. It looks best in front of a traditionally styled white wood home.

Charming and easy to install, the picket fence comes in various styles.
*Courtesy of Walpole Woodworkers*

A picket fence can come pre-assembled in panels or can be constructed onsite. Pickets can be straight, curved, or come to a variety of decorative points.

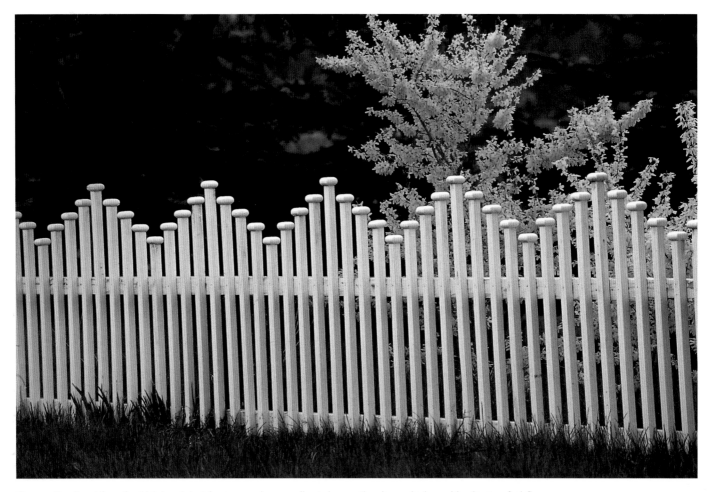

Generally about four feet high, picket fences make excellent decorative boundaries with plenty of airflow.

Picket fences are best used as decorative boundary markers.

Hydrangea, roses, clematis, and other flowers surround this picket fence for a softer enclosure. *Courtesy of Brian Cossari, ASLA – Hoffman Landscapes, Inc.*

Picket fences can be added to other structures. *Courtesy of Walpole Woodworkers*

Pickets and flowers are a great combination.

## Decorative Fencing

Many people wish to beautify their property with a decorative wall that gives privacy and/or enhances carefully placed and tended plantings.

Two houses were about fifty feet apart. To create a greater division between the two houses, one neighbor installed a decorative fence.

**57**

The second neighbor, the gardener, has reaped many benefits from this fence. Because of the flowers, the property is assumed to be hers.

*Long Hill, Beverly, a Property of the Trustees of Reservation*

*Courtesy of Siobhan Theriault*

Fences or walls can decorate a garden.

Fences and walls can frame views, create vistas, and provide perspective. *Courtesy of Siobhan Theriault*

Flowers are growing from the bike, which is quite a fence ornament in itself.

Many gardeners grow espaliers (es-pal-YAY), because of the interesting design that they add to their yards. The tracery of the branches against a barren wall becomes a graceful presence. Espaliers can also be used to create a living fence or screen, providing an elegant sense of privacy. You see espaliers in European gardens, where homeowners grow fruit without taking up much space. Many fruit trees can be trained into lovely, fruit-bearing espaliers.

Espaliers are an excellent way of turning a wall or fence into living art, concealing an ugly area (compost pile, garage), or creating a privacy screen without closing off the garden from light and air.

The espalier is a plant, which is grown flat, like a vine, against a wall, fence, building, or trellis. As such it has only two dimensions, height and width, while a normal tree has the third dimension or depth.

To create an espalier, pin or tie young, flexible tree limbs or vines to a wall or trellis in a symmetrical pattern or designs such as fan shapes, candelabras, fountains, diamonds and triangles. Completing a complicated pattern may take several years of pruning and shaping. Once the pattern is achieved, regular pruning keeps the plant properly shaped.

Of course, you must make sure that you choose a tree or plant that will not outgrow the area that you have intended. Your local nursery or gardening center can tell you about appropriate candidates for your yard.

*Courtesy of Siobhan Theriault*

# 4. PRIVACY FENCES

For many years, gardeners have been bringing the outdoors inside, but today the outdoors has been integrated into the home. Family rooms extend into porches and garden rooms: the indoors outside! A stonewall here, a meandering pathway, a hedge there, perhaps a nook and a cranny, and you can have a house surrounded by garden rooms. Some rooms might surround us with the flowers and perfumes of a garden. Others might focus on a flowing fountain or a playhouse.

These areas can give us a special, intimate place where we can relax and reflect, sheltered from the cares of the world. The breezes, the bird songs, and the feel of the sunshine are the reasons that an outdoor area is more than just that. It's an oasis from our responsibilities in the world. These whimsical and playful, spacious and cozy places provide a special place in time.

In the late afternoon or evening, we can sit back after the activities of a long busy day. The children might play flashlight tag or catch fireflies in a jar within the friendly confines of the yard, while the adults rock in their chairs, telling stories, watching the stars, even singing some songs. And slowly the lights of the night turn on.

As housing lots become smaller, these outdoor rooms can provide us with the feeling of space and light. The downside of this is the lack of privacy. In other words, we may enjoy chatting with our neighbors, but we might want to grill our supper without the whole neighborhood commenting. We don't always welcome the local dog or Frisbee player.

We also may want to conceal the air conditioner unit or our trash cans. By adding a privacy fence, we can transform our property into functional outdoor rooms without feeling visible to the entire neighborhood. A high solid fence is the usual choice, but a living fence or a thick row of hedges can also meet this need.

Privacy fences can block out the neighbor's yard, the noisy street (or the nosy neighbors), let us go outside in our pajamas, and enhance our feeling of well being. They can give us a sense of private space, block our property from view, and act as wind and sound barrier.

Unfortunately, since a privacy fence is more or less solid, it has a major impact on our neighbors, especially if it is built at or near the property boundaries. It can obscure the neighbor's view, blocks the sun or cooling breezes in your garden, ruining flowerbeds, or may come too close to a neighbor's house. For these reasons, municipalities often regulate fence design through building codes, often limiting their height, their "setback" from the property line, and even their appearance. In other words, in designing a fence, we should attempt to consider our neighbor's interests as much as possible!

*"Poor Henry, he's spending eternity wandering round and round a stately park and the fence is just too high for him to peep over and they're having tea just too far away for him to hear what the countess is saying."*
—W. Somerset Maugham, Cakes and Ale

An extension of your home, a privacy fence affects not just you but your neighbors. You can design one in a basket weave style, a picket-style, or a combination of stonewall topped with open fence, which provides some visibility over the top while allowing breezes to pass through.

*"A good neighbor is a fellow who smiles at you over the back fence, but doesn't climb over it."*
—Arthur Baer

*Langstraat Wood Inc., Seattle, Washington*

This fence helps to reduce noise pollution (including the sound of the snow plow!) from the street. It also acts as a good bank for the snow .

This Construction Heart security fence has a simple yet elegant board and batten driveway gate. The graceful top is trimmed with copper. Brick columns topped with copper capitals flank the gate, providing an imposing sense of arrival. *Courtesy of Tom Rider, California Redwood Assn.*

This privacy screen has several dimensions (i.e., wall, fence, trees), which gives it a definite advantage over just a fence.

This privacy screen is multidimensional. The trees are in front of the wall. A fence is behind them.

This attractive privacy screen has roses ascending its posts.

A plain board fence caps this stonewall.

Creativity abounds in privacy fences. A picket fence crowns this stonewall.

A series of redwood fence panels step along a sloping site. For more visual interest, the gabled "roofs" alternate with sections of 1x1 inch upright boards. *Courtesy of Barbeau Engh, California Redwood Assn.*

Blending with an existing arbor, this simple post and rail style fence offers both security and elegance. Design details such as the kickboard and the cap rail create visual interest. *Courtesy of Ernest Braun, California Redwood Assn.*

This Charles Prowell privacy fence is sectioned into two lower levels of solid floating panels. These are showcased with a flush-joined upper grid, serving to soften the sheer height of a nine-foot barrier. *Courtesy of Charles Prowell*

This classic six-foot tall basket weave fence marks the property line while providing privacy from nearby neighbors. *Courtesy of Tom Rider, California Redwood Assn.*

Built for a Victorian style home, this Construction Heart redwood fence has a dog-eared pattern to add visual appeal to an otherwise plain fence design. *Courtesy of Tom Rider, California Redwood Assn.*

A custom lattice topper and solid board fence mimic the barn-style garage doors on this Connecticut home. *Courtesy of Brian Cossari, ASLA- Hoffman Landscapes, Inc.*

A solid board fence of Construction Heart redwood divides and makes private a commonly shared yard behind a San Francisco duplex. Lattice top and finials add old-fashioned romantic charm. *Courtesy of Andrew McKinney, California Redwood Assn.*

The upper square design adds character to this post and board fence. *Courtesy of Mark Becker, California Redwood Assn.*

This board fence is a backdrop for the landscaping.

Flowers on the exterior side of the fence reflect those in the interior.

This Craftsman-style fence echoes both the Japanese character of the landscaping and the Craftsman elements of a classic shingle house. Fence boards are spaced apart so there is a visual connection between the sculpted plants and the garden within.
*Courtesy of Ernest Braun, California Redwood Assn.*

This solid perimeter fence and pergola allow privacy and protection, while the lattice fence top and gates preserve a certain airiness and a light motif. *Courtesy of Tom Rider, California Redwood Assn.*

This fence makes quite a statement.

This fence steps down the hill, allowing the passers-by glimpses into the beautiful garden.

*"Love your neighbor, but don't tear down your fence."*
　　　　*—Ukrainian proverb*

## Fences for Specialized Use

Designing and furnishing an outdoor living room is a popular home remodeling project. Outdoor living rooms often include a fireplace or firepit, cooking station, spa, and comfortable furniture. A fence is essential if your backyard is to become paradise. It can enclose an area, such as a spa, or define spaces for specialized use, such as a work area. Or it can camouflage the ugly air conditioner or the trash cans.

Your neighbor's property may be only ten feet away, but you can create a special place for your family. *Courtesy of Ernest Braun, California Redwood Assn.*

This redwood fence allows privacy while permitting air and light to filter through to an eight-foot spa and beyond to the master bedroom. *Courtesy of Tom Rider, California Redwood Assn.*

Two different fence designs are combined, providing both visual interest and privacy for a spa. The elegant lattice creates a decorative and airy screen, while the louvered screen provides privacy and wind protection. *Courtesy of Ernest Braun, California Redwood Assn.*

This redwood privacy screen surrounds a built-in spa. The intricate cutout keeps gentle breezes and filtered light flowing in the space. *Courtesy of Ernest Braun, California Redwood Assn.*

These attractive lattice fences conceal air conditioning units.

Hiding a bad view, such as these trash cans, is a practical reason for a fence.

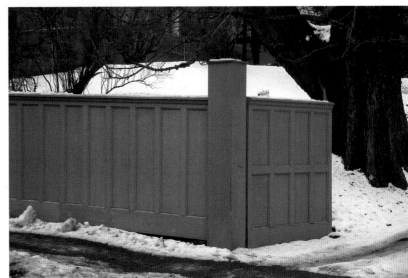

Here, fences provide children some privacy and perhaps prevent others from intruding in their play.

Stonewalls and a garden gate conceal a children's experimental garden. *Courtesy of Brian Cossari, ASLA- Hoffman Landscapes, Inc.*

This redwood screen features custom latticework and copper inserts that have been aged to a rich turquoise patina. It hides a garden tool area at one end of the patio. *Courtesy of Ernest Braun, California Redwood Assn.*

# Living Fences

Rather than using a built fence, you can use "green materials," which do not disrupt the natural surroundings. A living fence with its closely planted rows of trees or shrubs can be a practical and beautiful solution to the need for privacy. When plants and bushes are used creatively, the resulting "fence" appears to be a natural part of the setting. A smaller living fence can hide the unsightly such as the tool shed, the compost pile, or the garbage cans. Hedges, vines, and espaliers can also act as partitions to enclose or divide gardens and sitting areas.

This house sits on a busy intersection in a small town. The homeowner has designed a lovely area in the front but protected himself from the street noise and car headlights by also planting the arborvitae in front of the windows.

In addition to providing privacy, a living fence provides a habitat for birds and other wildlife, buffers traffic noise, and redirects the wind. Living fences are a good choice for many reasons. They last longer than other types of fences. Whether left to grow tall and untended or carefully trimmed, a living fence can serve as an attractive "green screen" that can create a virtually impenetrable barrier. Well-chosen and properly planted shrubs can offer security, privacy, and protection from the elements and beauty in all one package. Moreover, you don't have to paint it!

Since fast growing shrubs can provide a living fence quickly, you need to consider their ultimate height and the necessary setback from your property. If you can plant right on the property line, for example, your fence will eventually grown and extend into your neighbor's yard. Better to plant several feet away from the property line or cooperate with your neighbor in planning an adjoining hedge.

In considering a living fence, you should also consider:

- Are you looking for maximum privacy? Evergreens give you a year-around fence. An evergreen fence can be less formal and more interesting when you use it as a backdrop for some deciduous trees. By combining both varieties, you add depth and color variations.
- How high do you want it? Some shrubs have a large horizontal range while others tend to be more vertical.
- How formal do you want it? Neatly pruned evergreens tend to be more formal in appearance than deciduous trees.
- Are your proposed living materials susceptible to automobile fumes or road salt?
- What type of line do you wish to create? A straight continuous screen can be an attractive background for a flower garden, but a staggered hedge can create a windbreak or block a view.

This living fence is being planted on either side of the wall. The evergreens will grow high, providing more privacy.

This imposing living fence is a dense, formal border of evergreens, requiring regular shearing to maintain its rotund shape. *Hedge at Stevens-Coolidge Place, a Property of the Trustees of Reservation, photographed by Robert Evans*

It effectively screens the historic home from view. *Hedge at Stevens-Coolidge Place, a Property of the Trustees of Reservation, photographed by Robert Evans*

Vines are a versatile living fence that require little ground area. They can soften the harsh lines of a wall or hide an outdoor workspace from view. Ivy wall and hosta at Old Sturbridge Village photographed by Angela Kearney, Minglewood Designs. *Used with permission of Old Sturbridge Village*

Ornamental grasses can be used to define boundaries, screen views, and add color and texture to just about any landscape. Bamboo can grow into a sizable plant quickly, but you need to protect yourself from its invasive properties.

Careful selection of trees and shrubs combined with skillful design and routine maintenance can create landscaping accents that seem to belong naturally in their setting. This row of evergreens acts as a windbreak during the winter. *Long Hill, Beverly, a Property of the Trustees of Reservations, photographed by Robert Evans*

Many homeowners just let the natural environment take over so to screen their property from view.

Others try to make the living fence appear as natural as possible.

Living fences create food
and habitat for wildlife

Bushes and trees deflect the snow from this property.

A living snow fence can be beautiful throughout the year.

## Berms

A berm is an intentionally designed embankment or ridge composed of fill covered with loamy soil and plants to provide privacy to a home. A berm can be only a few feet or ten feet high. You can add even greater height by topping it with a fence or hedge.

This berm is under development.

A berm can serve as a privacy screen.

Sometimes it is landscaped.

A berm is a noise barrier constructed of earth.

Berms come in all shapes and sizes.

# NATURAL PLAYGROUNDS:

## Play Spaces That Cross the Boundaries of Ecology and Design

**Angela Seaborg, Minglewood Designs**

*Eat it, dig it, throw it — climb it, cut it, build it.* Expeditions in the woods reveal hidden keepsakes or peculiar pets. Wood, hammer, and nails result in a secret fort to share with friends. A long expanse of beach leads to magical castles and grand sculptures. Blank paper transforms into an airplane or pterodactyl, and an open area of lawn provides space to rest. These are the activities of childhood. The best learning happens when the imagination is set free. Natural playgrounds offer that freedom.

Looking affectionately back on my youth, I now understand how creative, unorganized play fosters an intrinsic sense of wonder and awareness. Together, with homeowners and communities, I cultivate landscapes that reflect upon natural systems to inspire unity, scale, and function. In so doing, each project is simultaneously responsive to the evolving palette of nature, the general design context, and the long-term goals of those experiencing it. By incorporating the variables of nature into design, children not only witness but also interact with the fundamental principles of our world. Natural playgrounds exemplify the unique relationship between ecology and design through their unconventional form and multi-functional use.

Natural playgrounds are not amusement or nature parks. They are not static features prescribed for a particular use. Natural playgrounds are ecologically designed landscapes that inspire open-ended play through the innovative use of ordinary forms. They are built on many scales, from the urban or suburban backyard to the schoolyard or community park. These play yards offer safety by forming inherent boundaries within creative design features. For example, a spiral perennial bed planted within the lawn maintains the color and texture of a conventional perennial garden, but it functions as a maze for young children. In the maze, kids feel a sense of security from the plants that encircle them, yet parents can unobtrusively watch from above. The perennial spiral can evolve over time with new and different plantings, or it can revert back to lawn once the kids have grown tired of it. On a larger scale, a mature sumac grove planted at the edge of a property provides screening and year-round interest from the house. It doubles as a living jungle gym. Natural playgrounds blend the technical design elements of texture, form, space, and boundary with existing landscape features such as water, topography, plants, and sun. The elemental components of these spaces change with weather, season, and light; these changes further expand the range of possibility for imagination. Most importantly, natural playgrounds stimulate the creative spirit of childhood.

The Legend Garden in Essex, Vermont, embodies the form and function of a natural playground. It encourages interaction with nature through exaggerated forms in a recognizable landscape. Built in a hay field for a traveling festival, the design features are intended to remain fluid. They are molded from existing elements on the property and can easily revert back to a functional hay field when the festival ends. Although designed as an independent feature of the festival, the meandering paths, plantings, and boulder gardens guide visitors discretely toward other areas of the festival. The primary feature of the garden is the Salamander Post. Rising up to five feet at its back and planted with thyme, it serves as a tactile wall that separates the woodland and open portions of the garden. Children can follow the stepping stones up the wall to achieve a distinctly different view into the woodland canopy. Older children might then make a connection between the salamander and its habitat.

Another feature of the Legend Garden is the Willow Weave: a meandering hedge made from the hanging bows of live willows. It outlines a "secret path" through which children can peer into the woodland beyond. The willow arbor, centered in the weave, is the gateway to the Salamander Post. The log walk builds control through concentration and balance in a fun, hopscotch form. Perennial wildflowers, depicted in yellow, produce a tangible fence along the paths.

The Legend Garden is a prime example of a natural playground. It illustrates how the thoughtful integration of ecology and design can stimulate the adventure of childhood. Natural playgrounds promote wonder and imagination. They offer discovery and independence within creatively defined boundaries. They are flexible and reactive. Natural playgrounds can be incorporated into any landscape. They can simultaneously accommodate collective design goals such as screening, privacy and noise reduction, safety and security. Natural playgrounds serve many functions through their unconventional form.

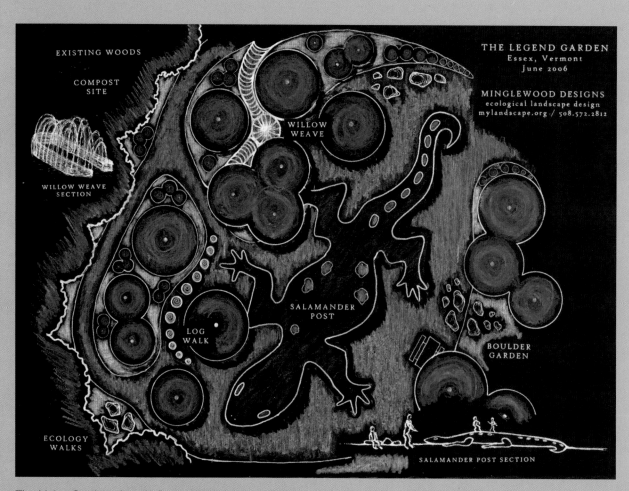

The Living Garden. *Angela Seaborg, Minglewood Designs*

# 5. SECURITY FENCES

When the children are big enough to play outside without you directly in sight but you want to keep an eye on them, when you get the new puppy, or when you want to discourage neighborhood children from cutting through your lawn, you might install a security fence. The purpose of a security fence is to protect your family and to discourage humans or animals from entering or leaving the designated area. Its height and edges can prevent property theft and vandalism, while its strength and placement can discourage trespassers or other dangers.

A security fence should be between six to eight feet tall, depending on your purpose. Although many types of fence can be used for security, local building ordinances may affect your allowable height and design. Certainly, you don't want to block a neighbor's view or obstruct a light source. An open design will allow air to circulate through your yard and prevent the fence from becoming the dominant feature in your landscape. On the other hand, if privacy is also a goal, you may want to consider adding a living hedge to your open design.

Security fencing options include:
• Wrought iron or metal fences
• Chain link fences
• Pool fences
• Wire fences
• Animal fences

## Wrought Iron Fences

Wrought iron, the classical example of ornamental fence material, has been used for many generations — even the ancient Greeks had beautiful ironwork. New Orleans, Spain, and South American cities are famous for their ornamental ironwork, which offers beauty, durability, and medium to medium-high security. A metal fence is difficult to cut, and the decorative tops make it difficult for a climber to traverse.

Although wrought iron fence is often used as a formal decorative fence, it also is used as a security fence. For security purposes, you'll want to be sure that the fence is sufficiently high; that the pickets are close enough together to prevent animals, children, or other intruders from fitting between them; and that the post and picket tops are designed to discourage individuals from climbing over the fence.

Ornamental iron fence can be wrought (or worked), cast, or machined. Using hammer and anvil, the blacksmith works the iron fence. Pouring molten iron into molds produces cast iron, and machined iron is milled directly from an iron or steel blank.

Ornamental ironwork is often termed "wrought iron," but today we have lighter and less expensive imitations in mild steel, composites, and aluminum. Given modern iron and steel manufacturing processes, the terms " iron fencing" and "wrought iron fencing" are generally used interchangeably. You can find pre-fabricated fencing or have fencing created for you.

Professionals normally install wrought iron fence because it requires metalworking and welding skills. Often, other materials such as brick, stone, or concrete are involved. Given the decorative quality of the fencing, any mistakes can be highly visible or can seriously compromise the fence's strength.

Rust is a problem with wrought iron. For years, rust-resistant paints have been available. More recently, fencing with powder-coat finishes that are helpful at resisting wear, weather, and color fading is obtainable. Ornamental aluminum is a lower maintenance option that has the same elegant Old World appearance.

*Courtesy of Walpole Woodworkers*

The aim of this Park Slope Design project was to design a private English style garden for this remodeled Cape Cod style home with new garage and guesthouse attached. Previously, the front of the home was totally exposed to the street. Now, wrought iron fencing and electric gates for the driveway and pedestrian gates have made it secure and private. Plantings hide the wrought iron fence, but you can see through the arbor and gate to enjoy the lush garden. *Courtesy of Joan Grabel/Park Slope Design*

Safety has to be the first priority when considering railings around balconies or decks.

One of the newer fences, this invisible fence, is much less visible than more standard fences. It adds grace, elegance, and safety.

Ornamental iron or decorative metal fences are available in many different styles and sizes. Of course, you can work with a metal worker to create your own using a model from previous generations or generating your own.

Decorative metal fence is often selected to enclose swimming pools. If you are considering wrought iron fence to enclose a pool area, be sure to check local building codes for fence height and between-the-rail spacing requirements. Also check your local zoning requirements to ensure that you are installing a fence that meets local zoning standards.

Ornamental fences are a work of art. They can be your garden ornament.

Ornamental fences can be in a color, white, or black.
*Field Farm Guest House, Williamstown, Massachusetts,
a Property of the Trustees of Reservations*

*"Fear is the highest fence."*
—Dudley Nichols

## Chain Link Fences

Chain link fence is often associated with such public facilities as swimming pools, parks, sports fields, and facilities. Many people use chain link fences to protect their property, children, and pets. Its light, airy appearance doesn't block the view, cast deep shadows, or affect the neighbors as much as most wood fences.

Today's new framework styles coordinate with black, green, and brown chain link to create a striking fence design, which can merge into the surrounding environment. The open weave of galvanized chain link allows people to see inside and outside the fence while providing security. Because of that same open weave, however, it offers little privacy. The insertion of slats into the galvanized steel wire mesh can provide partial privacy.

Because it is so flexible, chain link is a good option for varying types of terrain. It comes in a wide range of heights from a four-foot swimming pool enclosure size to twelve feet for basketball courts. Check zoning and building regulations before installation as there may be restrictions as to the height or type of fence that can be built.

A relatively inexpensive option, a standard chain link fence provides low to medium security. Bolt cutters can cut its mesh, which supplies easy climbing handholds and footholds. A mini-mesh chain link fence is less easily climbed or cut.

The fabric, or the diamond-shaped steel wire, that composes the fence is important in determining its strength. The lower the gauge number, the thicker the galvanized steel wire and the more expensive the fence will be. The steel is often coated with zinc or aluminum for protection from rust. The framework and gates have to be sufficiently strong, and the fittings sufficiently protected to keep the fence looking as new as possible.

This chain link fence is adorned with wisteria.

This chain link fence is stark.

**101**

This fence screened with bushes and vines conceals a basketball court.

## Pool Fences

The phone rings. The supervising person has decided to mow the lawn, manicure his/her toes, vacuum, or do something other than watch the child.

Children are fast, curious, and able to slip through small spaces. The U.S. Consumer Product Safety Commission found that over three-quarters of the children drowned in residential pools had been seen five minutes or less before being missed and subsequently discovered in the pool. Most of the victims are under three years. A large percent of drowning incidents occurs while one or both parents were responsible for supervision, and more than half occur in a pool owned by the child's family.

Fences and secure gates are the best way of preventing mishaps and keeping unsupervised children out of trouble. To prevent climbing, the fence should be at least four feet high with no nearby objects that would assist the child in climbing over. To prevent crawling under or squeezing through, the fence bottom should no more than four inches above ground. The fence gate latch, which should be out of a child's reach, should be self-closing and self-latching.

The rolling hills of Connecticut remain on view through this paddock style fence. A safety mesh on the outside of the fencing meets Connecticut Pool Code. *Courtesy of Brian Cossari, ASLA – Hoffman Landscapes, Inc.*

The corridor of open grid panels created by Charles Prowell Woodworks are scattered with etched glass to create a defined entry. *Courtesy of Charles Prowell*

To demarcate the boundaries between an entry foyer and a pool terrace, Charles Prowell Woodworks designed repeating open grid panels and gates to diffuse the weight of the overarching arbor. *Courtesy of Charles Prowell*

A perennial garden of orchestrated bloom and a safety fence enclose this poolside. *Courtesy of Brian Cossari, ASLA – Hoffman Landscapes, Inc.*

**103**

The aim of this Park Slope Design project was to create different garden rooms, connecting a grassy area to a large pool in the rear of the property. The wrought iron fencing not only provides for pool safety but also creates an aesthetic division and support for various vines. The arbor suits the scale of a large rear pool and Provencal-inspired garden design. *Courtesy of Joan Grabel/Park Slope Design*

A good pool fence needs to prevent children from crawling under, climbing over, or squeezing through the bars.

This large pool has both a lattice fence and a wrought iron fence. *Courtesy of Walpole Woodworkers*

Pool fencing is about safety and scrupulous adherence to all legal requirements. Beyond that, most people want a fence to provide privacy for the pool area.

Experts agree that pool fencing should have, at least, the following characteristics:

- At a minimum, fence height should be four feet. Higher fencing is available, but you need to consider the fact that if a child can climb a four-foot fence, he's usually able to climb a five foot one as well.
- If swimming pool fencing is picketed, the fence pickets should be spaced four inches or less apart, with no rails (horizontal cross-pieces) that allow the fence to be climbed. For mesh fences, the largest openings should be no more than 1 3/4 inches wide.
- The fence should allow easy visibility through it to the pool area. To prevent the climbing child from falling directly into the pool, the fence should be installed away from the water's edge
- Fence gates should be self-closing and self-latching. Ideally, they should open away from the pool or outward. Their latches should be lockable.
- If a doorway or window in the house leads directly to the pool area, the opening should be considered part of the pool safety fence and have an audible alarm device.

This self-closing, self-latching gate protects the pool. Note the privacy fence in the background.

Security fences can be most attractive. A Mercer Island arbor brings the bold architecture of the home into the garden space while its image reflects from the pool's surface. *Langstraat Wood Inc., Seattle, WA*

## Wire Fencing

Fences were an essential element of American life for our forebears. They delineated property lines, kept out unwanted visitors, and kept in livestock. Homeowners constructed fences or barricades from available materials such as wood, stone, or living fences of densely grown shrubs or trees. In New England, they were built primarily of stones; in the South, they were constructed from timber.

As the country was settled, however, and settlers pushed westwards, traditional fencing material was not available to meet their needs. Some regions did not have a ready supply of fieldstone or trees to be turned into fences. Smooth wire was not strong enough to prevent cattle from wandering. Without a suitable, inexpensive fencing option, a homesteader in the Plains and Texas territories could not safeguard his crops. He had to have a fence to keep wild and domestic animals out of the fields and to keep livestock enclosed, to serve as a field perimeter or as a pasture divider, and to safeguard his property. Since fencing usually represents a rather large investment, it is especially important to select a fence that is affordable, easy to maintain, durable and, most importantly, works as planned.

Around 1874, someone developed barbed wire in or near DeKalb, Illinois, located on the edge of the prairies. This cheap, low maintenance fence with its incorporation of barbs and smooth wire would "keep the varmints away." Barbed wire was less expensive and more effective than other options. The manufacturers developed "more merciful barbs and shorter prongs," which helped to facilitate settlement of the West. The farmers fixed boards to the wire in order to give it greater visibility and prevent injury to the livestock.

Before the advent of barbed wire, few Texan cattlemen acquired land on which to graze cattle. Cattle roamed the range – much of which was still public lands – and cattlemen drove their herds of wild Texas Longhorns over the long trails to railroad stations or northern ranges.

The influx of homesteaders to the area meant that the open land was fenced off. Barbed wire was the tool that made it easier for the settlers to occupy the public lands.

Fences made for healthier herds. The animals were enclosed and no longer had to roam for feed and water. Consequently, the herds increased – not only in number but also in weight.

In their effort to protect the public lands and their way of life, some cattlemen cut the fences, hoping that this would force the homesteaders to leave "their" land. This night-time fence cutting led to violence and even death. Ultimately, laws were enacted to protect those who erected fences and punish those who illegally tried to prohibit the lawful and orderly settlement of the area.

*"This is the finest fence in the world. Light as air. Stronger than whiskey. Cheaper than dirt. All steel, and miles long. The cattle ain't born that can get through it. Bring on your steers, gentlemen!"*
—John W. Gates (wire salesman)

By the end of the nineteenth century, the old way of life in Texas was gone. Open range ranching was transformed to closed range ranching. The long cattle drives would eventually be abandoned in favor of the railroads. The invention of barbed wire created great changes in the American frontier. It made such an impact that as of 1991 there is a Historical Museum of Barbed Wire and Fencing Tools in McLean, Texas.

Barbed wire is still used today on farms and ranches.

*A fence should be horse high, hog tight and bull strong.*
—*Source unknown*

## Animal Fencing

Today's animal fencing is designed to either confine animals and to prevent pets and wildlife from entering or leaving the area. The type of fencing needed depends on several factors including animal species, age, and breed. Fencing should be strong, well supported, and anchored so it cannot be bent or pushed over. Its height and ground clearance should prevent animals from trying to jump over or under them.

In deciding upon an option, the height and strength of the animal need to be considered. You certainly don't want an animal to crash through it, nor do you want paws or hooves to become ensnared. Wire mesh, or woven wire fence has a variety of wire gauge, mesh size, and height. Highly visible to the livestock, it is useful for both enclosure and protection.

Electric fence is a more expensive option and can require maintenance, but it has less impact on your view. Electric fence is designed to deliver a quick shock to animals and predators that come into contact with it. This type of fence can be used in a stand-alone mode or can also be used in conjunction with other fences (board fences and suspension fences come to mind). It works particularly well with containing livestock and delivers a quick shock to predators that contact it.

Sometimes an electric fence is used in conjunction with existing fencing. With this setup, creatures approaching a garden brush against electrified wire and receive a harmless shock, discouraging the animal from proceeding further. These fences are child-safe, although the child that touches the wire will receive the same harmless jolt that an animal would.

As more towns institute a leash law, dog owners are searching for a way to exercise their dog safely. With a wireless fence system, the dog wears a special battery-operated collar with a radio receiver. The dog is trained to understand that if he wanders past the defined perimeter and hears an audible beep, he will receive a harmless static shock. The invisible system relies on a wire that demarcates the area where the dog is to be contained. The wire is buried in the soil, run along existing fences or along building foundations. The perimeter wire generates a radio signal that activates the collar as the dog approaches.

The yellow sign warns that this fence is electrified.

*"There is something about jumping a horse over a fence, something that makes you feel good. Perhaps it's the risk, the gamble. In any event it's a thing I need."*
—*William Faulkner*

Board fence has two to four rails between posts. Generally, this fence is constructed in wood, but recent advances in PVC fence construction make this a viable alternative. Fences of this type are also constructed of steel pipe, usually featuring a durable powder coating finish. In addition, concrete manufacturers produce sturdy and aesthetically pleasing post and rail fence.

Bull and Fence at Old Sturbridge Village photographed by Angela Kearney, Minglewood Designs. *Used with permission of Old Sturbridge Village.*

Sheep can safely graze here.

So can cows.

Horses can be injured if the fencing is not highly visible. A four to six feet high board fence, which has two to four rails between posts, is traditionally used.

The fencing must be sturdy or you will be repairing and replacing it more than you wish.

Today, Bambi is no longer beloved. Suburban homeowners are fighting off deer who like to eat their prized rhododendron and flowers. Deer don't like to jump high and wide simultaneously. Consequently, a six to eight foot fence can keep deer away from your garden as long as you plant some shrubs or trees in the prospective landing zone.

A popular fencing is a flexible, black plastic 2-inch mesh that is attached to fence posts or directly to trees around the perimeter of the property. If the fence does not completely surround your property, the deer will just find another path to your appetizing landscaping.

When selecting fencing, be sure the mesh is small enough to discourage the deer, but large enough so that a foot or paw does not get stuck in the mesh.

The flexible plastic deer fence is just visible behind the attractive metal gate, which signals humans that they are venturing into a fenced area.

Alpine style stone piers and a custom driveway gate keep the deer out while defining the style at the entrance of this contemporary home. *Courtesy of Brian Cossari, ASLA – Hoffman Landscapes, Inc.*

# 6. GATES

Gates are a means of access. They act as doors to the property; they are an opening through a wall, fence, or hedge; they prevent visitors from entering or exiting where they shouldn't. They also can be an augury of what is to come.

When selecting a fence for your property, you generally need to choose an appropriate gate. The gate should be functional, decorative, and complement your fence – whether it is metal, wooden, or vinyl – and your property.

You can opt for a basic pre-fabricated gate or have one custom designed to make a statement or meet a specific purpose such as vehicular traffic. You can choose one that opens manually or one that has an automatic opener for security and privacy. You can install the remote-controlled sentries at the end of a driveway or add them to an existing wall or fence. Today, homeowners, who want more control over who has access to their property, can use their wireless handheld devices to open their gates from anywhere.

You can personalize your gate by adding a special gate latch or decorative hinge. You can use adjacent plantings to help it harmonize with your landscape.

You can install the gate yourself, hire a local handyman, or hire a home garden services fence/gate installer.

*"The world is all gates, all opportunities, strings of tension waiting to be struck."*
*—Ralph Waldo Emerson*

At the beginning of the twentieth century, wrought iron gates and fences symbolized good taste and a certain class. Often imposing, they can make a strong initial impression on visitors about the gardener and the garden they are to meet. These beautiful gates are certainly designed for grand entries.

Beautifully crafted iron gates can be found throughout the generations.

*Gate at Stevens-Coolidge Place, a Property of the Trustees of Reservation, photographed by Robert Evans*

Courtesy of Brian Cossari, ASLA – Hoffman Landscapes, Inc.

*"If you only knock long enough and
loud enough at the gate, you are sure
to wake up somebody."*
—Henry Wadsworth Longfellow

Gold leafed spear tips and repoussé gold leafed pineapple transform the design of this aluminum gate from simple to sophisticated. *Courtesy of Martell's Metal Works*

This old gate leads us to further gardens. *Gate at Stevens-Coolidge Place, a Property of the Trustees of Reservation, photographed by Robert Evans*

This hand-forged gate from Martell's Metal Works reminds you of the early twentieth century wrought iron gates that symbolized good taste and a certain class. *Courtesy of Martell's Metal Works*

Hand-forged and hand-painted humming bird and morning glories give the Morning Glory Gate its unique look that will compliment any yard or garden. *Courtesy of Martell's Metal Works*

Martell's Matunic Gate is simple but elegant. Its hand-forged steel and satin black finish makes this gate suitable for many entrances. *Courtesy of Martell's Metal Works*

This entry gate with its hand-forged steel and stained glass design extends a welcome and sense of security to its visitor.

A simple gate may lead us on to a new path. See detail below.

The clear All Heart entrance gate has pounded copper detailing and redwood pergola. *Courtesy of Charles Calister, Jr., California Redwood Assn.*

A soaring multi-canopy tops this sapwood-laced fence and gate. The ends of the trellis boards are artfully shaped to add design interest. The double gate boards are placed diagonally to create an eye-catching entry. *Courtesy of Andrew McKinney, California Redwood Assn.*

This double gate uses architectural grade Clear All Heart redwood. Posts, topped off with capitals, support the weight of the gate. *Courtesy of Ernest Braun, California Redwood Assn.*

Craftsman-style boundary fence and driveway gate include upper railings styled in a concave shape and alternating sizes of upright fence pickets. The iron strap hinges are handmade. *Courtesy of Tom Rider, California Redwood Assn.*

*"Still round the corner there may wait a new road or a secret gate."*
*—J. R. R. Tolkien*

The designer chose smooth-textured Construction Heart redwood for this entrance to a 1930s' shingled house. The delicate porthole and arch add further contrast to the rough textured fencing. *Courtesy of Clyde Eagleton, California Redwood Assn.*

*Courtesy of Siobhan Theriault*

This boundary line fence prevents passers-by from walking on the lawn. The window boxes soften the line. *Courtesy of Charles Callister, Jr., California Redwood Assn*

*Courtesy of Siobhan Theriault*

*Courtesy of Siobhan Theriault*

A gate and lamps tempt the curiosity of viewers as to what is inside of this private property. *Courtesy of Brian Cossari, ASLA – Hoffman Landscapes, Inc.*

This gate protects the private road to the beach.

When you consider your outdoor area from a vertical perspective, you have endless opportunities to be creative.

This garden gate by Charles Prowell Woodworks complements the long stucco boundary wall. *Courtesy of Charles Prowell*

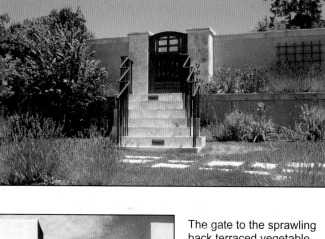

When approaching the property, you have this view. Note the terraced design of the walls. *Courtesy of Charles Prowell*

The gate features etched glass inserts with a blockish grid meant to complement the solidity of the front perimeter wall and zigzag staircase. *Courtesy of Charles Prowell*

The gate to the sprawling back terraced vegetable gardens invites passers-by to pause and peer within the fortress of the surrounding privacy wall. *Courtesy of Charles Prowell*

A lovely entrance. Old Sturbridge Village photographed by Angela Kearney, Minglewood Designs.
*Used with permission of Old Sturbridge Village.*

Summer sun and the driveway entrance gate create interesting shadows. *Courtesy of Brian Cossari, ASLA – Hoffman Land-scapes, Inc.*

A solid, multi-paneled double gate by Charles Prowell Wood-works is set against the natural materials of a desert stucco pil-lar and the partially exposed Camelback Mountain in Phoenix, Arizona. *Courtesy of Charles Prowell*

# Appendix A: Resources

The **Brick Industry Association** or BIA is the national trade association representing distributors and manufacturers of clay brick and suppliers of related products and services. Its mission is to promote clay brick with the goal of increasing its market share and to safeguard the industry. Specifically, it renders technical assistance to architects, designers, builders, and consumers; provides marketing assistance to the industry; monitors and positively influences governmental actions; and provides other member services. The BIA website contains technical information on brick fences and landscaping applications as well as other uses for brick.

    1850 Centennial Park Drive, Suite 310
    Reston, VA 20191-1542
    703.620.0010
    www.gobrick.com

Quality landscape architecture requires building materials that are beautiful and long-lasting. Materials need to withstand environmental elements yet retain their symmetry and aesthetic purpose. Redwood performance characteristics include resistance to shrinking, warping, and checking in addition to durability. This means redwood projects age beautifully. Decks, fences and shelters made with redwood simply look better ten, fifteen and twenty years after construction. Equally important, there are cost-effective redwood grades to specify for every project, whether it is a public plaza or a residential garden. **California Redwood Association** can help you find your fence.

    405 Enfrente Dr., Suite 200, Novato, CA 94949
    415.382.0662
    info@calredwood.org
    www.calredwood.org

Founded in 1977, **Charles Prowell Woodworks** designs and produces custom interior and studio furniture for discriminating clients in and around San Francisco. In 1995, its founder, Charles Prowell, turned to a long neglected genre—the garden gate. He has created a line of custom wood driveway gates, fence panels, lighted columns, arbors and pergolas, and porch railings that are designed with the same care as his furniture. His designs withstand the changing seasons for generations and complement the architecture of a thoughtfully designed landscape.

    San Francisco, Chicago, Boston, Boise, and Baltimore
    978.474.9000
    www.prowellwoodworks.com

Joan Grabel is a landscape designer located in Studio City, California. Previously an exhibiting painter, Joan transferred her artist's sensibility from the canvas to the landscape and founded **Park Slope Design** in 1986. Specializing in custom residential gardens, integrating landscape and architecture, Joan works closely with clients to actualize their vision. She has been featured on Home and Garden Television and in various publications.

    3940 Laurel Canyon Blvd. #173, Studio City, CA 91604
    818. 788. 4312
    parkslopedesign@aol.com
    www.parkslopedesign.net

**Hoffman Landscapes**, founded in 1987, is a full service landscape design, construction, and management company. Brian S. Cossari, ASLA, is a national award-winning landscape architect licensed to practice in Connecticut and New York. The company's services include master design plans by landscape architects, supported by a staff of botany and arbor experts.

    647 Danbury Rd., Wilton, CT 06897
    203.834.9635
    brian@hoffmanlandscapes.com

**Langstraat-Wood Inc**. is a landscape design build firm based in Seattle, Washington. It strives to look at each site and each client as a new opportunity for inspiration. Its goal is to expand its personal frame of reference so that it will have more to bring to each new project rather than a slight variation of a previously conceived pattern. The firm is committed to remembering that once all the design professionals and installation crews leave, the client is left with what has been created.

    816 NW 49th St., Seattle, WA 98107
    206.547.6710
    www.langstraatwood.com

**Martell's Metal Works** displays creativity in a wide variety of forms: gates, railings, furniture, accessories and more. The designs range from Old World to contemporary to whimsical. Martell's Metal Works is known for excellent craftsmanship and attention to detail. Skilled artisans create handcrafted one-of-a-kind work from various metals, including steel, aluminum, stainless steel, bronze and copper. Its motto is: "If it can be imagined, we can create it" turning 2-D concepts into 3-D reality.

    36 Maple Ave., Seekonk, MA 02771
    508.761.9130
    blksm@aol.com
    www.matellmetal.com

Angela Kearney, principal of **Minglewood Designs**, runs a landscape design and planning firm dedicated to creating harmonious garden environments for residential and community clients. Each land-use plan combines Zen garden design principles with the ecological and environmental character of the region and site. Sensitive site planning and attention to detail define its work.

34R Lincoln Rd., Wayland, MA 01778
508.572.2812
www.mylandscape.org

**Old Sturbridge Village,** a museum and learning resource of New England life, invites each visitor to find meaning, pleasure, relevance, and inspiration through the exploration of history. With a 200-acre living history museum at the center of its collections, exhibits, and programs, the Village presents the story of everyday life in rural New England from 1790-1840, during the first 50 years following the American Revolution. The museum is located off Route 20 in Sturbridge, Massachusetts.

1 Old Sturbridge Village Rd., Sturbridge, MA 01566
800.SEE.1840
www.osv.org.

**Rossington Architecture** is a full-service architectural firm dedicated to excellence in design and project management. Founded in 1999, the firm's work focuses on residential projects, including additions, renovations, new homes, and multi family housing. The work derives directly from its context, taking clues from existing conditions and carefully interpreting the needs of the clients and focusing on how they use the spaces they occupy. Detailing is kept purposefully clean, simple, and timeless.

4529 18th St., San Francisco, CA 94114
415.552.4900
phil@rossingtonarchitecture.com
www.rossingtonarchitecture.com

**The Trustees of Reservations (Massachusetts)** are more than 40,000 people who want to protect the places we love, secure our landscapes and landmarks for future generations, or who simply like getting outdoors. Together with its neighbors, the Trustees protect the distinct character of local communities and inspire a commitment to special places. It offers access to new experiences and endless opportunities to connect with the people and activities that make life rich, rewarding, and fun. Its passion is to share with everyone the unique natural and cultural treasures that it cares for. With nearly one hundred special places across the Commonwealth, the Trustees invite you to find your place.

572 Essex St., Beverly, MA 01915-1530.
978.921.1944
www.thetrustees.org

For generations, **Walpole Woodworkers** has offered homeowners choices that enhance the style of front yards, back yards, and gardens. Some decisions may be practical — a fence around a pool or tennis court, for example — others, purely aesthetic. The firm has quality choices and options from fence to pergolas that will surely enhance the joy and pleasure felt every time approaching one's home or stepping outdoors for fun and relaxation.

800.343.6948
www.walpolewoodworkers.com

# Appendix B: Fence Maintenance

*"Tom appeared on the sidewalk with a bucket of whitewash and a long-handled brush. He surveyed the fence, and all gladness left him and a deep melancholy settled down upon his spirit. Thirty yards of board fence nine feet high."*
—Mark Twain, Tom Sawyer

Stonewalls can be vandalized and hurt by humans and machinery. Metal can rust, and wooden fences require painting. Like most of our household items, fences and walls need maintenance.

With its formal look, metal is a popular choice. The wind won't topple wrought iron, but it does need to be properly painted or sealed. Rust-resistant aluminum and stainless steel do well outdoors – especially when given a powder-coated finish –which means the color is baked on.

Many prefer wood for a fence. The downside is that wooden fences are exposed year around to sun, rain, snow, rot and insects. Some woods, including redwood, cedar or pressure-treated pine will survive quite well, but there is a certain level of maintenance needed to keep them attractive.

Now, as Tom Sawyer knew, few things are as pretty as a nice white fence, but those nice white fences can fade after several years. If you plan to paint your fence, expect to invest lots of time scraping, sanding, priming, and repainting every five to seven years.

You can use exterior semitransparent stain. When this durable finish fades, you can usually paint right over it without sanding or scraping.

Most fences are painted or stained, but paint is a mixed blessing. There are few things as pretty as a freshly painted fence – or as ugly as a peeling one. For best results, always scrape, sand, or power wash to remove loose paint; then prime the bare wood; and finally apply the best-quality exterior paint you can afford.

Finally, never apply a clear topcoat finish, such as polyurethane varnish or shellac, to an outdoor project. Sun and rain will eventually blister the finish, leaving you no choice but to sand the entire surface and start again from scratch.

To keep your wood fence looking new, experts recommend:

- Using hot-dip galvanized metal, aluminum, or stainless steel fence fasteners to resist corrosion. Nails should have a ring or spiral shank to reduce the chance of loosening.
- Treating the surface with UV inhibitors soon after installation. UV light is why fences turn grey, so ensure the presence of an inhibitor.
- Brown stains at the nailing points of cedar and redwood fences can be removed with Trisodium Phosphate (TSP). Black stains at the nailing points are more successfully tackled with an oxalic acid solution.
- Chlorine bleach is effective against mildew, fungi and in removing much of the grey oxidized layer generated by exposure to UV light.

Luckily, maintenance-free vinyl fences are available today. They come in several colors and a wide range of styles, including picket, basket weave, three-rail, and lattice.

A vinyl fence does not require painting or staining. It only requires an occasional power washing. Many have a 20-year warranty against peeling, flaking, rusting and blistering. Since they are sold with integral fasteners, there are no screws, nails, or splinters. If it has UV protection, your vinyl fence should last forever.

One drawback to vinyl is that it can become brittle with age and cold temperatures, and it can fade and dull in the sun. Should you need a replacement piece you have to get it from the manufacturer.

Rust can destroy a beautiful fence.

*"Sighing, he (Tom) dipped his brush and passed it along the topmost plank; repeated the operation; did it again; compared the insignificant whitewashed streak with the far-reaching continent of unwhitewashed fence..." Mark Twain, Tom Sawyer.*

*"Every wall is a door." Ralph Waldo Emerson.*

**128**